The GEM Connection

Team Cohesiveness for a Diverse and Multi-Generational Environment

Connie Cwik

DEDICATION

This book is lovingly dedicated to my Mom, Shirley Dobbins. She was an incredible role model for me and taught me to never give up, be consistent in all your endeavors and persist no matter what. She also taught me that my Faith would sustain me when nothing else would. She was a great businesswoman and a good friend to many people. She never met a stranger and always was kind to everyone she met. I am proud that she was my mother. I hope I have made her proud with this book. Unfortunately, we lost her to cancer in 2016 but her legacy lives on.

CONTENTS

FOREWARD   i

1   COMMUNICATION SKILLS - THE KEY TO INFLUENCING PEOPLE,   1
INCLUDING YOURSELF

2   MANAGING WITHOUT WORDS – BODY LANGUAGE OR   11
NONVERBAL COMMUNICATION

3   BUILDING AND MAINTAINING RELATIONSHIPS   20

4   INFLUENCING PEOPLE: THE ART, SCIENCE, AND PRACTICE   26

5   MANAGE THE MULTI-GENERATIONAL GAP   36

6   MENTAL MAPS: UNDERSTANDING HOW YOUR MIND WORKS   47
SO YOU CAN UNDERSTAND OTHER

7   THE BASICS OF CORPORATE POLITICS   54

8   DEFINING YOUR LEADERSHIP SKILLS   61

9   BE THE CHANGE EXPERT   69

10   INTO ACTION; INTEGRATING THE SKILLS   73

FOREWARD

As I was working on this book, the title just kept eluding me. Then, while I was preparing for a presentation to a local networking group, it occurred to me that what I do is like connecting paper clips of all sizes, shapes, colors and ages. Team cohesiveness, cross-teaming and communications across multiple generations is very much like connecting these paper clips. As a professional and executive coach, that is EXACTLY what I do! I help businesses build better teams and talent across multiple generations and multiple teams.

When talking to my good friend, Susan about the title, she asked me the question, "Do you know the original manufacturer of paperclips?" She had learned the answer watching Jeopardy!

I did the research and the answer to that question is GEM! That is how the book got its name and why the paper clips are on the cover.

It is my hope that you will get some valuable tips that help you and your teams perform at a higher level. Enjoy!

CHAPTER ONE:

COMMUNICATION SKILLS - THE KEY TO INFLUENCING PEOPLE, INCLUDING YOURSELF

In corporate America today, networking and relationship building skills are paramount for managing your career because there is so much cross-teaming and multigenerational communications efforts that need to be put into it. As I was preparing to write this book, I realized how amazed I have been by the lack of relationship building being taught in business programs today. Companies spend a significant number of dollars presenting training and career development programs that focus on technical skills and improving weaknesses, but few focus on the art of relationship building and communications skills.

Building relationships is the MOST important skill you can develop to build a career. Often, people move up the corporate ladder because they have associated themselves with the right people. If you contribute in a way that helps your manager or your boss get promoted, it almost assuredly means that you will move up with them. If you are in a small business situation, you can benefit substantially from helping the owner grow and build the business.

You can also significantly impact your upward career path by "managing up" with other executives within the company, outside your business unit and outside the company.

But how do you make the right decision about who to "hitch your wagon" to? The primary consideration is to make sure you choose someone who is on the fast track to where you want to go. Knowing what it is you want from your career, as well as what your 5-10 year goals are, is critical in making the right decision. There are no right or wrong answers regarding where you want to be in 3, 5 or 10 years; only honest ones. You must be blunt with yourself about your ambitions or lack thereof, otherwise, you will find yourself heading down a path you have no motivation to follow.

Having good communications skills is also very important to being a good team leader as well as a team member. You must be able to communicate with many types of people. If you are like most people, you may need to hone your skills in this area so that you can adapt your communication style to other's style. This will enable you to be much more effective at leading and participating in a team situation.

There is a direct correlation between good communication skills and a successful team leader. If you look around at the people that have been most successful you will find that they have one thing in common. They are good communicators and have been clear about the direction of the team. These folks have used the power of influence to build their teams in a way that ensures continued success. They are authentic in their communications and in their style.

Whether you are in a corporate environment or own a small or medium sized business, communications skills are a vital skill that will lead to more success when building a team.

Rapport

Think of a time when you met someone and you instantly felt a connection with that person. What was it about them that caused you to feel that way? You just met them, so how could this be? One of the reasons for this feeling of connectedness is the *rapport* that was established.

How valuable would it be to establish this type of rapport with new or prospective team members the first time you meet them? Would it be of even greater value to have a repeatable process that would help you do so time and again?

Everyone has heard the saying, "You never get a second chance to make a first impression." There has been no truer quote because there has never been a truer statement. If you are meeting new teammates for the first time, it is critical that the first impression is a positive one.

So, let's explore how we go about making sure that first impression is one that you will both remember positively for years to come. Establishing rapport is the first and most basic skill that you will want to develop.

What is rapport? Rapport is the ability to be on the same wavelength and to connect mentally and emotionally with another person. It is the ability to meet people where they are, to build a climate of trust and respect. It is essentially meeting individuals in their "model" of the world and not yours. Establishing rapport does not mean that you have to agree, but that you understand where the other person is coming from. This happens through matching the cues - verbal, eye movements, and body language - that the other person is expressing.

Rapport works best when it becomes second nature and a way of dealing with people *at all times.* Having rapport as a foundation for any relationship means that when there are issues to discuss, you already have the groundwork in place that will make it easier to talk those issues through and thus prevent those issues from developing into complaints, objections, or problems.

When creating rapport, it is important to mirror the person with whom you are communicating. To do so, it is important for you to be open to your intuition. You can train yourself to build and refine this skill because you do not want the other person to think you are mocking them. To mirror someone else you simply have to match their breathing, sit the way they sit and use some the same gestures they use. So if someone is sitting forward in their chair with elbows on the desk, then you at least sit forward in your chair. Use your discretion as to whether or not you put your elbows on the desk. In another example, if someone tilts their head to the right, then you might tilt your head to the left. Remember, you are mirroring them!

If you can, let your senses kick in to help you. This will provide you with the ability to see, hear, and sense external changes in their body language. You will also be able to notice minor cues, both verbal and nonverbal, exhibited by individuals with whom you are communicating. This is the first step to eliminating any internal responses that may cause us to try to be a mind reader. Many of us try our best to read other people's minds by thinking we know what they are thinking without reading the cues because we are closed off to our intuition. So trust your intuition, open up your senses and learn to read the clues that others are providing.

Rapport is one of the keys to the ability to influence. If we are going to influence people on our team or another team, then it starts with rapport. It starts with acceptance of the other person's point of view and their style of communication. To influence someone, you must be open-minded enough to appreciate and understand that person's standpoint. But it works both ways: I cannot influence you without being open to influence myself.

Rapport is also integral to building trust. Rapport is achieved when two people see each other's viewpoints, appreciate each other's feelings, and are on the same wavelength. We all have different maps of reality – ways in which we perceive our world and when we feel understood, we give people our trust and open up to them more easily.

One of the easiest and quickest ways to establish rapport is to find anything, no matter how small, that you have in common with someone. You might ask them where they are from and then mention something that you know about it. Or perhaps you both have a similar career background and can relate to each other that way. The key is to find something that you have in common by asking questions and listening to the answers.

Building Trust

"To be trusted is a greater compliment than to be loved." – *George MacDonald*

"If you don't trust people, people will not trust you." – *Lao Tzu*

Let's define trust. Merriam-Webster defines trust as "assured reliance on the character, ability, strength, or truth of someone or something; or one in which confidence is placed."

Mutual trust is a shared belief that you can depend on each other to achieve a common purpose. So really trust is the willingness of one party to be vulnerable to the action of another party. You have the expectation that the party will perform that action without you having to monitor or control the person. Basically I'm saying that trust is letting go of control and believing the action will be taken.

People sense how you feel about them. They will know if you trust them or not. They may not realize it consciously but they will just know that something is "off". If you want to change their attitude toward you, change any negative attitudes you have toward them. Building relationships requires the building of trust. Trust is the expectation that people have that they can rely on your word; it is built on integrity and consistency in relationships.

Feeling heard is very important in a team situation. If people feel like you are listening to them, even if you disagree, they will respect you as a leader. If you listen well, people will trust you.

Let's go back to rapport for a minute, and ask yourself, "Do you remember a time when you met someone and liked them instantly?" That probably happened because that person asked you open ended questions and then just listened to your response. Once they heard something that resonated, then they added something to the conversation. They heard something they could relate to.

You cannot establish trust if you cannot listen. A conversation is a relationship. Both speaker and listener play a part, each influencing the other. Instead of being a passive recipient, the listener has as much to do in shaping the conversation as the speaker. This is a critical skill to achieve and practice at all times. Nothing makes someone trust you more than knowing that you are actively listening to them and that you are interested in what they have to say.

Let me give you contrasting examples. Have you met someone and you tried to have a conversation with them, but you could just tell by their closed body language that they were not listening or hearing anything that you were saying? Then you met someone else that was engaged, really seemed to be listening and as you're talking, they're nodding their head. Maybe they are even asking you a few questions about what you're talking about.

The second person is using effective listening and demonstrating that they are engaged. The first person gave you the impression that they are not at all interested in what you are saying. The two behaviors elicit very different responses from us and one establishes rapport while the other does not.

You also need empathy. Empathy is the ability to put yourself in someone else's shoes to better understand their experiences. It allows us to create bonds of trust and gives insights into what others may be feeling or thinking. It helps us understand how or why others are reacting to a given situation. Having empathy can sharpen our "people acumen" and inform our decisions. Empathy is also important in a team environment. It helps to take the emotion and judgement out of a given situation. This is very important when problem solving or trying to resolve conflict or issues.

When you think about all those things, empathy then is putting yourself in someone else's shoes. Empathy is not judging someone but instead trying to understand where they are coming from. It will change the way you perceive them and the way you communicate with them. It will also elevate their opinion of you.

Trust-based working relationships are a MUST in today's workplace. Trust plays an important part in your organizational success and the success of your team efforts. Trust elevates levels of commitment and sustains effort and performance without the need for management controls and close monitoring. Trust between a manager and an employee is based on both parties' perception of the other's ability, goodwill, and integrity. If you have this type of relationship, then each of you will have the expectation that the other is supportive of your efforts and that you have each other's' backs. You can establish and nurture trust-based working relationships with almost everyone that you work with.

Let me give you an example of that. I was responsible for leading a large global team at a major software company. We conducted quarterly planning sessions, and everyone knew that when we joined that meeting, we were all equal. The rule was, there are no "bosses" in the room. Each person was free to contribute with complete honesty, authenticity and transparency with no fear of retribution or fear of judgement. This team was recognized as one of, if not the most effective team within the organization. In order to solve problems and create the best strategy for our client, we had to leave egos at the door and have a trust-based working relationship. This did not mean that we always agreed or that there was never any conflict. Of course we disagreed vehemently at times, there were heated arguments and EVERYONE felt heard. What we DID NOT do was make it personal. We all understood that great solutions would come from this type of authentic interaction and conflict. We all realized and respected that we had different ideas about things. Our motto was "We all have different ideas. They are not right or wrong ideas, only different!"

These types of relationships take work and time to build. I am not one that believes that it takes a long time to build but more importantly it takes consistency in your demonstration of integrity. Always keep your word and you always have to hold others accountable for keeping theirs. That means that if you tell people that they should feel free to bring ideas to the table and then you shoot them down, then you lose all credibility. So take the emotion and judgement out of dealing with others as much as possible. This is the foundation of building trust.

In many situations, you must make an effort to extend trust when it is not reciprocated. This can make you vulnerable and uncomfortable, but in a critical business situation, it can mean the difference in success or failure.

Of course, there are situations where you have to be selective in how much trust you put in someone else or even how much information you will share with them. I'm not saying you should be a completely open book. That's not at all what I'm suggesting, but you can be selective in how much you trust and with what information. This can happen when you suspect that the other party may stab you in the back or may not be trustworthy themselves.

If you find yourself in this situation you should be mindful of how much information sharing you are willing to do with this person and make that decision beforehand. You may consider only trusting them just enough to get through the project successfully and that's OK so give yourself permission. It is important in this instance to be very factual in your communications and keep a "paper trail" of communications.

Often if one person does not trust another, there are underlying issues that come into play. At one point in my career, I was thrust into a situation of having to work with a person that was obviously very under-qualified to do the job they had been assigned. It was difficult for me to trust that person to get the job done while at the same time they were not very trusting of anyone. Clearly, the underlying issue here was insecurity caused by being in the wrong role.

I realized that I had to find a way to work with that person without jeopardizing the job that had to be completed. It was apparent to all of the members of the working team that this person's insecurities and lack of trustworthiness were a problem.

I chose to take the high road and eventually won this person's trust. I did that by keeping my communications all about work, factual and as helpful to the other person as I could.

In the end, this person chose to move on to another position that better suited them. Had I not been patient and worked hard to earn a trusted working relationship the entire team would have been negatively impacted. I was able to keep stability on the team by demonstrating leadership. This was accomplished by making sure that tasks were assigned to this individual that they could complete. That way he was at least contributing to the team efforts, which made him feel a part of the team and the team did not get resentful.

As you can see, trust can be a source of competitive advantage. Trust-based working relationships are an important source of your continued competitive advantage because trust is valuable, rare, and cannot be substituted or imitated. The level of trust a leader can garner from his or her employees is contingent upon the employees' perceptions of the leader's ability and integrity. Be mindful of the fact that your integrity will impact all aspects of the team. It will also impact cross-teaming efforts and how other teams perceive you, your team and it's trustworthiness.

A recent Gallup worldwide study of employee engagement to determine whether trust could be a source of competitive advantage showed that trust is significantly related to sales, profits, and turnover. More broadly, the study concluded that the ability of a general manager to earn higher levels of trust from his or her employees most likely creates a competitive advantage for a firm over its rivals. That's how important rapport, listening skills, empathy and trust have become.

CHAPTER TWO:

MANAGING WITHOUT WORDS – BODY LANGUAGE OR NONVERBAL COMMUNICATION

"Start to notice your body language, and other people's, and see how much you can pick up about what someone is saying just by watching them." – Russel Webster

Why are we talking about managing without words in the team environment when verbal communication is so important? When building a team, your non-verbal communications will be the first thing that prospective team members will notice about you. If you are working to build the best team possible, then why not make sure that your non-verbal communication is just as effective as your verbal and/or written communication?

Body language can help you connect - or not connect – with people on your team. You may look the part, exude confidence, and act assertively, but if your body language is saying something else, then you may miss the connection. All of us intuitively can tell if there is incongruity between body language and the words being spoken. If you can read someone else's body language, then you can look beyond what people say to what they mean. We unconsciously give clues as to what we mean by simple gestures, facial expressions, or eye movements. We all give those clues away.

The same can be said for your tone of voice. If your tone does not match your words then there will be a disconnect between them. Your audience will notice and will either be confused by the mixed messages or will question your authenticity.

Remember your attitude is infectious and drives behavior. Your attitude is the one of the first things people pick up on in face-to-face communication. Attitude is really a combination of body language, tone and physiology! Just as laughing, yawning, and crying are infectious, attitude is infectious. Before you say a word, your attitude can infect the people around you with the same behavior.

You will always notice attitude. Think about this: two people enter the room. One of them is looking down with a frown on their face and walking slowly. The other comes in walking briskly, with a big smile on their face with good posture. What would you think about each of their attitudes? Right. And, BOTH of them are infectious! Plus it gives clues to other people about how to approach them.

Our physiology can betray our thoughts by using our body language and tone to reflect in our movements what we really believe about a given situation. The good news is that you can change your state of mind by simply changing your physiology!

Take a moment and try changing your physiology. If you are sitting, stand up. If you are slumped, sit up straight. Make some minor adjustments to your physiology and you will notice a definite and definitive change in your state!

That's why you need to know what your body is saying. Body language accounts for more than half of what other people respond to and make assumptions about when they are connecting with you. More often than not, you're not even consciously thinking about it. But by becoming conscious, you can put yourself 50% ahead of the game. Pay attention to your body language and be deliberate about it. For instance, if you are nodding your head "Yes," but saying the word "No," the person you are communicating with will read the body language of "Yes" instead of the word you used. We automatically sense the incongruity of the movement versus the words.

Try this. Watch people and their body language. Does it match with what they are saying? How does that impact your perception of them? When watching TV or a video or even in person, look for any incongruencies in what people are saying vs what their bodies are doing. They usually will not even realize they are doing it!

That is nonverbal communication. You cannot NOT communicate anything! Try to sit for one minute without speaking. Even if you can keep from moving, you will still communicate rigidity, anxiety, or something. We are always sending messages and communicating something.

It is important to observe and try to understand what is being communicated. In many situations, people say what they think intellectually rather than what they feel emotionally. There is some truth in the old cliché "actions speak louder than words." Body language, carefully observed and interpreted, can tell a lot about what others are feeling.

Nonverbal communication is learned and often practiced on an unconscious level. We attract people by using these nonverbal signals, and sometimes those we attract (or who are attracted to us) are unwholesome.

Our body language can be disguised behind a mask made of a fear of rejection. For instance, have you ever been in a situation when you felt a little insecure? You may become stilted or even "act" differently just to hide your insecurity. Often we should down emotionally or "close" our body language by crossing our arms over our chest or leaning away from others.

On a personal level, think of a time when you wanted to ask someone out on a date. You might put on a mask of indifference or try to hide your feelings if you felt your invitation may not be accepted. This can discourage wanted and needed relationships from developing. Those who want and need to develop certain relationships must relearn their nonverbal skills and unmask themselves to avoid alienation. All I'm saying is that we need to become somewhat vulnerable and be more open and natural. We want to reflect our true intent in the situation better.

Body language is as open to misinterpretation as verbal communication is. It must be interpreted in the context of one's lifestyle, family, cultural background, and other factors that may be obscure. Each person has a limited repertoire of gestures and uses the same gestures to signify certain feelings. Gestures also can occur in clusters, so that while any particular gesture alone may not mean much, when it is reinforced by other gestures in a cluster the feeling or attitude being projected is confirmed.

Are you using open or closed signals? With your body language, you're constantly saying either, "Welcome, I'm open for business," or, "Go away, I'm closed for business." You may be showing that you are an opportunity or a threat; a friend or a foe; confident or uncomfortable; telling the truth or spouting lies.

When you are operating from inside a genuine attitude such as enthusiasm, curiosity, or humility, your body language tends to take care of itself and sends out unmistakable signals of openness. Nonetheless, there are things you can consciously do to make sure you're showing your best face. If you want to show that you're open for business, a friend and not a foe, without saying a word, then you have to open yourself up to the world in the first second of every encounter. Open body language - together with open facial expressions – includes uncrossed arms and legs, ease in facing the person, good eye contact, smiling, standing or sitting erect, leaning forward, flexible shoulders, and a generally relaxed aura. Open body language makes expressive use of hands, arms, legs, and feet.

Our gestures often tell something about us that we are not able or willing to communicate verbally. "Open" gestures are present when a person is ready and willing to communicate, while "closed" gestures are present when there may be something standing in the way of honest and complete communication. These gestures can be observed in spousal relationships, parent–child relationships, supervisor–worker relationships, worker–client relationships, and any other time that two people are communicating. Maybe you will discover that your body language has been "telling" on you! (Appendix B contains a partial list of "open" and "closed" gestures .")

How do you or others come across nonverbally? If you are struggling when communicating with someone, then take the time to understand why that is happening. We often get lazy and just do not explore the reasons this could be happening.

When your communications are challenging with someone you can quickly improve that communication by asking yourself some questions to better understand why you are challenged.

Is the message I am saying the message I am feeling? In other words, are my words, tone and body language matching up with my feelings. If I am happy, is that the message I am sending? If not, then make a quick adjustment so that your happiness comes through.

Am I hearing what the other person is saying? When someone else is talking, are you really "hearing" what they are saying or are you trying to interpret it or are you formulating your response before they are even finished talking? You will be amazed at how much more you will "hear" what others are saying if you just pay attention to everything they say then respond.

Is this person someone with whom I am interested in communicating? This is an important question to ask ourselves if we are struggling. If our answer to this question is negative then why not? Until you can get to the answer to this question, you will not be able to effectively communicate with this person. Are there emotional barriers? Are they the wrong audience? There are any number of answers to this question and you need to be sure you actually have a desire to communicate for the right reasons.

Does this person want to talk with me? Often we assume that others want to have a dialogue with us and this is not always the case. If we determine that a person does not want to talk with us, then until that changes open communication will not be possible.

Would I like to disagree with this person at this time? Does this person want to disagree with me? If there is a sense of disagreement, then stop and address the disagreement. You will not have effective communications unless you discuss disagreements directly. This can actually be the very catalyst that drives open communications going forward.

Am I overreacting to what this person is saying? Does this person overreact to my statements? If the reactions do not match the communications, your best option is to neutralize the situation as quickly as possible. Get to the bottom of why the overreaction and address it honestly and directly.

You can use these questions when in a situation that you may be unsure about. It will help you better understand what is happening nonverbally pretty quickly so that you can adjust. These are just a small sampling of the questions you should ask yourself. Be creative and ask questions of yourself if you sense any issues with your communications with others.

Make yourself comfortable with the other and don't invade their personal space. Avoid being too close or too far away physically. (Within two feet is a comfortable range.) We all joke about "close talkers" and it is one of the most uncomfortable situations for a lot of people. Be respectful of others' personal space.

Be relaxed and attentive with others when communicating with them. To gain acceptance or rapport lean slightly toward the other person. Avoid slouching or sitting rigidly as we have discussed before.

Maintain frequent eye contact with others especially when shaking hands. However make sure you are not staring, glaring, or looking away. It is really uncomfortable for the other person if you stare (maintain eye contact too long) at them so avoid this if possible.

Give nonverbal communication while the other is talking, such as a simple nod of approval. This is also called "active listening" and sends a clear signal that you are listening to what they are saying and that you are interested in what they are saying.

Keep gestures smooth and unobtrusive. Don't let them compete for attention with your words. Avoid letting your gestures reveal emotional frustration. Many of us "talk with our hands" so make sure that your hands are saying what you want them to say!

Your rate of speech should be average or a bit slower. If you normally speak at a fast pace you will need to modulate your speed and tone so as not to move too quickly. If you normally speak more slowly then you will need to pick up you pace to keep some people engaged.

Avoid sounding impatient or hesitant and control the tone of your voice. Like we have already discussed your tone is very important to effective communication. You should avoid sounding cold and harsh.

Stay alert through long conversations. This can be challenging if you are not fully engaged so be aware of this. Closing your eyes and yawning blocks communication!

Our facial expressions also play a role in our nonverbal communications. "Face values" are based on facial behavior. What causes you to make one facial expression more often than another? We usually only have a few facial expressions that are repeated, so when you know what they are, you can easily read just about anyone you ever meet. In poker, this is called the "tell." This is sometimes called a micro expression. We all have a "tell" or two that show up unconsciously to let people know more about ourselves than we realize. (See Appendices A & B.)

People who are in rapport unconsciously synchronize their body language and their verbal characteristics. When you deliberately synchronize your body language with another's, amazing connections can happen. Our response to synchronization is a function of our predisposition to reciprocate behavior. It's hardwired into the human brain. This is commonly called "mirroring" or "matching." For instance, if the person you are interacting with crosses their legs then you should cross your legs so that you are portraying a mirror image.

This has become so automatic and ingrained for me that I do it without thinking about it. Last year I was in client meetings in Norway and had been with my British client the previous two days. Everyone in Norway thought I was British! They were surprised to learn that I am a Southern American! It was natural and automatic and completely non-threatening.

There are two core questions about body language. What signals are you sending about yourself? What emotional feedback are you giving others in response to the signals they are sending to you? Challenge yourself by asking these questions and more importantly answering them. Evaluate the response you are reading in others when you interact with them. Do this in every situation of your life and you will begin to notice an automatic adjustment of your body language and because of this you will enjoy very effective communications and therefore much more success in your relationships! Let's talk about building relationships.

CHAPTER THREE:

BUILDING AND MAINTAINING RELATIONSHIPS

"The most important single ingredient in the formula of success is knowing how to get along with people." – *Theodore Roosevelt*

Building relationships is an important key to your personal success. Successful people have the ability to develop relationships that last. Building relationships require the building of trust. We discussed this at length in Chapter One.

Your relationship with yourself is your closest and most important relationship. What kind of relationship with yourself have you chosen? Have you chosen a judging relationship? Are you a coach to yourself? Are you fearful, or loving?

What kind of friendship do you want with yourself? This may seem silly but we need to treat ourselves well. Do you want an inner friend that judges you or denies you love? Or, do you want an inner fiend who accepts you just as you are?

These are difficult but necessary questions because we do this unconsciously. It's all built on our filters and experiences from our childhood, from our hurts and happiness, from our successes or failures, and from our relationships. All of these come together to impact our relationships. As we are building relationships with others, those relationships will be built on the relationship we have with ourselves.

We need to balance giving and receiving in our relationships. Your life can only be in balance when giving and receiving are in balance. Every interpersonal relationship is built on this fact of life. The person who always gives, acts against this principle just as much as the person who only takes. This basic truth is valid without exception, everywhere that we deal with people. Life doesn't go very well when you fail to strike a healthy balance between the two. And it goes the opposite way as well. If you ae always taking and another person is always giving, the person taking could create stress in the relationship. Or they may not be guilty, because the giver is trying to control the situation and does not let the other person give.

Remind yourselves of love and translate the word "love" into action, because that is the basis of harmonic relationships and gracious giving and receiving. When giving and receiving are in proper balance, you have time both to listen and to tell, to help others and to receive help, to be there for people in need and to ask people for something.

Do you ask the question, "How much do I have to give before I receive something in return?" Be clear about the answer to this question and set the appropriate boundaries.

"Think once before you give, twice before you take, but a thousand times before you ask for something." – Marie von Ebner-Eschenbach

Get interested in people and show your appreciation. Think of the way you'd like to be remembered by those around you and give of yourself accordingly throughout the year. Practice a random act of kindness every day. These little moments, over time, have a huge impact. I challenge you to practice this. It doesn't take a lot of effort, but the reward is immeasurable. The added benefit for you is that you'll be in a more positive frame of mind overall. Commit to one or more of these, right NOW! Your relationship building skills will soar!

"You can make more friends in two months by becoming interested in other people than you can in two years by trying to get other people interested in you," advised Dale Carnegie. Resolve to focus your energy on helping others feel valued and appreciated. Show your appreciation with a thank you or a smile. Call up someone you haven't spoken to in a while, just to catch up on how they are. If you have children, give one child at a time your full attention for an afternoon. Write a note of appreciation to someone who is important to you

A relationship is two people eliciting responses from each other. That means you have to have a dialogue; not just via email and not just via text. If you want a different response, then you must change your own actions. Have a real conversation. Real problem solving requires a back and forth dialogue. In my coaching practice, we talk about having authentic conversations. You don't have to be confrontational to have a direct and honest conversation with someone. As a matter of fact, they will appreciate you and your initiative. If you want a change in response, then you must change your own actions.

As a business professional, you should ask yourself, "What business am I in?" The answer is quite simple: if your business has anything to do with people - and ALL businesses do - you are in the business of building relationships. Some people think if they sell "things," they are in the business of selling. They aren't. They are in the business of building relationships – because that's how you sell things. People still do business with people. Those in management are also in the business of building relationships because that's how you get things done.

You have to learn to be a person of influence not only for your team but other teams as well. In today's world we MUST practice cross-teaming to achieve our goals in corporate America. In small business you must partner with others to fill in any gaps in your services. All of this requires you to be good a relationship building.

Everything is so interconnected. If you have a milestone to reach on a project, and that milestone is dependent on another team to achieve their milestones first, then you should help that team. If you build a relationship by helping them reach their milestones, then you have built positive political capital and escalated your reputation. We are dependent on people who are members of teams. Therefore, relationship building is a MUST to achieve your goals.

Working relationships can often turn into friendships outside of work. There have been numerous studies conducted regarding employee engagement. One of the things that creates/maintains engagement at work is if you have a friend at work. It also gives people a reason to look forward to going to work. They will be less likely to let their team down. Having friends mitigates the physiological consequences of stress because you can share the risk.

When you are building relationships you should take preferred personality and communications styles into account when working with co-workers. To work effectively with people, take their preferred style of interaction and decision-making into account. Many misunderstandings and conflicts derive from differences in style.

For example, "Perceivers" may see "Judgers" as unwilling to take the time to explore creative options. Conversely, "Perceivers" who may stray from the agenda can irritate "Judgers." "Dominance" may perceive that "Influencers" pay too much attention to their intuition. "Visuals" may perceive that "Kinesthetic's" take too much time to think about it while "Auditories" think there is just too much noise.

Remember that differences do not make the other person wrong, it only makes them different. No matter what assessment or theory you use it is important to get an understanding of how to relate to others in their preferred style of communication. The responsibility of communication lies with the communicator, not the recipient of that communication.

If you are not certain how to do this, please contact our office and we can assist you with an assessment or some individual coaching to help you determine your style and how to determine the style of others.

If you want to build a high performing team, you must build a diverse team. To be effective managing and motivating a diverse team you will need to have the relationship building skills outlined here.

Building business relationships are paramount to your long-term success. Research shows that even with the best products and business practices, you still need strong relationships and networks to succeed in this marketplace. The following is a guide to turn personality differences and conflicts into positive business results.

Respect is at the core of building business relationships whether internally or with clients. It is the glue that holds together the working order of teams, partnerships, and managing relationships. (Up and down, peer-to-peer, internally and externally.) Respecting the right to disagree is a concept like apple pie and motherhood. We all "buy into" it, but can we truly cultivate it? I take the approach that I can learn something from everyone I meet. This keeps my ego in check and also shows respect to the other person.

The first step is to identify the specific areas where you have differing opinions. Many people see things in terms of black or white, right and wrong. "It's my way or the highway." "If you don't agree with me then you must be wrong." When a situation is viewed with this attitude, a power struggle ensues. When, however, a situation can be seen with an acceptance of another's personal view and a position is simply a matter of opinion, not fact, then collaboration and compromise is possible.

Identifying and understanding a diversity of opinion allows people to shift their attitude to one of compromise and negotiation. I have a strongly held belief that I am entitled to my opinion. I also strongly believe that you are entitled to your opinion as well. These opinions may be different; not right or wrong. This will allow you to have the attitude of compromise and collaboration.

Respect leads to accepting a person for what he or she is. Accepting a person and their opinions, where they are, creates an environment of trust. Trust, leads to a willingness to be open to new opportunities, new collaborations , new strategies, new ideas and new products.

Once you become willing to adopt an attitude of acceptance and understanding, you can begin to avoid power struggles, which drain energy and limit your effectiveness. You relationship building will get stronger and you will realize more success. Now that you have relationship building skills, how do we influence people?

CHAPTER FOUR:

INFLUENCING PEOPLE: THE ART, SCIENCE, AND PRACTICE

"Pull the string, and it will follow wherever you wish. Push it, and it will go nowhere at all." — Dwight Eisenhower

"Before you can inspire with emotion, you must be swamped with it yourself. Before you can move their tears, your own must flow. To convince them, you must yourself believe." — Winston Churchill

Every hour of every day, at every level in every organization, influential people succeed and non-influential people don't. It is imperative that you learn how best to influence others in a professional environment. You hear a lot of talk about gaining consensus in corporate America today, and you can't accomplish that without the ability to influence others. To truly be successful you have to learn the art of influencing people.

"Knowing others is wisdom, knowing yourself is Enlightenment."
- Tao Tzu

The first step to influencing others is self-awareness. Great leaders, coaches, and communicators don't focus solely on their followers, players, and audience. They have a high degree of self-awareness. We all have basic skills to lead, coach, or communicate; unfortunately, most of us have a few psychological blocks when it comes to applying those skills well and consistently. Knowing yourself will help you overcome your own blocks.

Awareness is the first step in the process of influencing others. As you grow in self-awareness, you will better understand why you feel what you feel and why you behave as you behave. That understanding then gives you the opportunity and freedom to change those things you'd like to change about yourself. Without fully knowing who you are, self-acceptance and change become impossible therefore making influencing others next to impossible.

Having clarity about who you are and what you want (and why you want it), empowers you to **consciously and actively** make those needed changes. Otherwise, you'll continue to get "caught up" in your own internal dramas and unknown beliefs, allowing unknown thought processes to determine your feelings and actions.

Do you know what your beliefs are? Our beliefs impact and affect every aspect of our lives including our professional lives. We seem to just go through life without evaluating what we believe and even how those beliefs impact our success. Did you know that you may hold a strong belief that is limiting your success? In my coaching practice we spend time understanding our strongest beliefs. We almost always find more than one belief that is limiting us in some way.

Many of our beliefs have been formed and developed even from an early age. The good news is that we can change our beliefs once we realize they are limiting us.

There was a time in my life when I realized that my fear of failure was causing me to be way more cautious than I needed to be. I had a belief that if I failed people would judge me negatively. Once I realized this, I was able to work hard to change that belief to a more empowering belief. Now I believe that there is no such thing as failure, only results.

The difference changing this belief has had on my willingness to put myself out there the try new things has been amazing. Now when I try something that doesn't work, it doesn't feel like failure. I am just get feedback through results! I can change my strategy and try again using a different approach!

You can do the same thing if you take the time to write down your beliefs. As you do this, make sure that all of them are supporting your goals and are empowering. If not, change them. If you need help doing this, contact my office to find out how to work with me.

"Persuasion is the art of getting people to do what you want them to do, and to like it." – *President Eisenhower*

The power of persuasion can mean the difference between success and failure. It can help you get more of the things you want faster than anything else. It can guarantee your progress and enable you to use all your other skills and abilities at the very highest level. Your persuasion power will earn you the support of others. One word of caution here is that you must be correctly reading their agreement and then get verbal confirmation. Too often people leave a meeting believing they had persuaded the other person to their way of thinking or to buy into their idea when in actuality they did not. Always verbally confirm it. Then send an email to all parties concerned that outlines the agreement that you all just made. Give the recipients the opportunity to agree again in writing or to offer any changes as they recall them. This way you not only verify agreement but you also have documented the agreement.

There are always two choices: either you can persuade others to help you, or you can be persuaded to help them. It is one or the other. Most people are not aware that every human interaction involves a complex process of persuasion and influence. And being unaware, they are usually the ones being persuaded instead the ones who are doing the persuading.

The key to persuasion is motivation. Every human action is motivated by something. Your job is to find out what motivates other people and then to provide that motivation. People have two major motivations: the desire for gain or pleasure and the fear of loss or pain. The desire for gain motivates people to want more of the things they value in life. They want more money, more success, more health, more influence, more respect, more love, or more happiness. Human wants are limited only by an individual's imagination. No matter how much a person has, he or she still wants more. When you can show a person how he or she can get more of the things they want by helping you achieve your goals, you can motivate them to act on your behalf.

People are also motivated by the fear of loss. This fear, in all its various forms, is often stronger than the desire for gain. People fear financial loss, loss of health, anger or disapproval of others, loss of love, and the loss of anything they have worked hard to accomplish. The reason people fear change, risk, and uncertainty is because these things threaten them with potential losses.

Whenever you can convince a person that by doing what you want them to do, they can avoid loss or receive gain, you can influence them to take a particular action. The very best appeals, however, are those where you offer an opportunity to gain pleasure and an opportunity to avoid loss or pain at the same time.

Recently a coaching client recognized the need to get help and was motivated to do the hard work. Why was that? His boss convinced him that coaching would help him understand better what he wanted from his career and how to get there. It would also keep him from being put on probation and possibly losing his job. He was offered an opportunity to grow his skills and keep his job at the same time. This is clearly a dual motivation!

Influencing people is not about being phony or acting like someone you are not; it's about creating a favorable link between your internal nature, with its beliefs and values, and the external world where you go to work. Yes, use your imagination and be creative in the way you connect with people by intuitively adjusting your style to others. You can easily do this without losing yourself if you will trust in the process and in who you are. It will help you maximize the potential in every relationship, be it personal, business-related, or social.

As I've already said, you cannot influence someone unless he or she likes you in some way. That is why rapport is the key to influence: to influence, you have to be able to appreciate and understand the other person's standpoint.

People are motivated for their own reasons, not yours. One of the golden rules of the therapy profession is that everyone needs at least one person with whom they can openly and unashamedly discuss every little detail – happenings, desires, fears – of their life, whether it is from the past, present, or future. There are other psychological needs, too – to be accepted unconditionally, appreciated, recognized, respected, desired, valued, approved of, or complimented. All these things affect the way we communicate with each other. Listen carefully, ask questions to show that you are genuinely interested, and you'll be amazed at the power of being a good question asker and a good listener. You will have far more influence when people think you are interested in them.

You cannot influence others if you cannot listen. A conversation is a relationship. Both speaker and listener play a part, each influencing the other. Instead of being a passive recipient, the listener has as much to do in shaping the conversation as the speaker.

We all know people who dominate meetings by excessive "babble" that causes a lack of productivity. This impacts every person in that meeting. Keep in mind that each person at the meeting has a different set of values, processes information using different modalities, and moves at a different pace. If you learn to be cognizant of this and respectful of each individual, you will be perceived as an effective listener. Always remember that just because someone communicates differently than you does not make them wrong or stupid - merely different!

Often we have too much difficulty listening to other people because we employ barriers to effective listening. We "know" what we are going to hear so we make assumptions and formulate an answer without really listening to the other person. We are seeking confirmation of our point of view and not information from the other party.

Often, what's being said is getting in the way of what *needs* to be said. This happens in meetings when someone really has nothing substantive to share but just rambles on about something unrelated. Before you know it, time is up and another meeting has proven to be unfruitful.

One way to break down the barriers is to use active listening skills. Active listening involves playing back your own interpretation of what has been said in acknowledgment – "As I see it, what you mean is..." This confirms for others that you are listening and ensures you hear the true meaning behind what they are saying. If there is a discrepancy you are giving them an opportunity to clarify their position. This just increases your effectiveness and allows for more influence.

Another way is being able to consciously take a different perceptual position during communication (especially in negotiations) is a valuable skill. It gives you more information about a situation and much greater flexibility in your point of view. It helps you appreciate the influence of your verbal and non-verbal behavior on others and improves your understanding of other people. It creates a level of trust, credibility, and respect that is difficult to shake.

Taking different perceptual positions enables you to step out of what you are currently experiencing and gather new information by seeing things from a different perspective. You can also check out how your own words and behavior may be impacting other people, and how they may be feeling about you and your actions. This new knowledge will help you make the necessary changes in your behavior and thus achieve the desired outcomes.

There is not a right way, nor is there only one way, to influence others. Everything and I do mean *everything*, is a factor in influencing people.

And we are, all of us, at all times, influenced by people, places, events, and situations. Sometimes we are affected more or less by these things, but we are continually influenced by what happens around us.

So what about the specifics in the workplace? Your job requires you to influence people nearly all of the time. It may take the form of gaining support, inspiring others, persuading other people to become your champions, engaging someone's imagination, or creating relationships.

Whatever form it takes, being an excellent influencer makes your job easier. An interesting point about people who use their influencing skills well is that other people like being around them. There's a kind of excitement, buzz, or sense that things happen when they're around.

This is because they don't sit around wishing things were different while moaning there's nothing they can do about it. They don't sit around blaming others or complaining about what needs fixing. They see what needs doing and set about getting it done.

Truly excellent influencing skills require a healthy combination of interpersonal, communication, presentation, and assertiveness techniques. It is about adapting and modifying your personal style when you become aware of the effect you are having on other people, while still being true to yourself. Behavioral and attitude changes are what's important, not changing who you are or how you feel and think.

You may try to exert your influence through coercion and manipulation. You might even succeed in getting things done that way, but it isn't really influencing. That's forcing people to do what you want, often against their will. You'll never succeed in winning support that way. Pushing, bullying, bludgeoning, or haranguing DO NOT WORK! And like elephants, people don't forget. They will remember the experience.

Indeed, if you force someone to do something without taking their viewpoint into consideration, the impression that experience creates is how they will see you *forever*. You're stuck with it unless you deliberately change what you do in order to be seen differently. And that's ten times harder to do than creating a good impression in the first place.

People are far more willing to meet you halfway (or more) if they feel acknowledged, understood, and appreciated. They may even end up doing or agreeing to do something they wouldn't previously have done because they feel good about making the choice.

Influencing is about understanding yourself and the effect or impact you have on others, or don't have on others. Though the primary relationship can, on occasion, be one way, it is almost always two-way, and it is about changing how others perceive you. In other words, the cliché "perception is reality," makes perfect sense in the context of influencing. It doesn't matter what's going on internally for you - if the other person doesn't perceive it, then it doesn't exist (other than in your own mind).

You could be making the most brilliant presentation ever, but if you haven't brought your 'audience' with you, the brilliance is wasted. The difference is in being able to see what's going on for *them*, which will be different from what's going on for you, however much you may have in common.

Influencing can sometimes be looked at as the ability to 'finesse' – it's almost sleight of hand. The other person isn't prodded into seeing your view of the world but is persuaded, often unconsciously, into understanding it. Sometimes you can get so used to your own personal style or way of being, or pattern of communicating, that you don't consider how it is being received, so you don't think of behaving any other way.

Influencing is about being able to move things forward - without pushing, forcing, or telling others what to do. One of the most powerful forces affecting people's behavior is the avoidance of humiliation. No one wants to embarrass themselves if they can help it. So changing your behavior entails a certain amount of risk. But if that behavior change is deliberate and you have made an effort to see the world from the other person's point of view, then humiliation can be avoided on *both* sides.

Whatever the arena you work in, influencing others is about having the confidence and willingness to use yourself to make things happen. Influencing people is also the ability to 'work' a dynamic, whether it's a large group, one-on-one, or over the phone. By 'working' the dynamic, we mean using every means of communication at your disposal - both verbal and non-verbal - to create the impact you want rather than simply letting things happen.

Next let's explore how to become influencers and build teams in a multi-generational and diverse culture in your company or organization.

CHAPTER FIVE:

MANAGING MULTI-GENERATIONAL AND DIVERSE TEAMS

Regardless of what you may think, there are lots of commonalities between the generations. You see, I believe everyone wants to succeed, regardless of what generation you're in. Everyone wants to feel valued and feel like they've added value to the workplace, to their family, and to their relationships. Nobody likes conflict. Some people deal with it better than others, but no one really likes conflict.

I also believe that everyone, regardless of when you were born, wants clearly defined goals and objectives. We all need clear communication. And I think everyone likes to have fun and enjoy their work. You see, there are lots of commonalities between the generations. I think it's a myth that none of us have anything in common. I also think there are way too many generalizations used when talking about the different generations. Yes, we need to understand the differences but we also need to understand the similarities.

There are five distinct work groups, and let's briefly talk about them

Traditionalists or Silent Generation

You have your traditionalists, or what some people may call the matures, the silent generation, the veterans. They were born before 1945, and they're 72 years of age or older. They make up 3.7 million of the workforce, or somewhere thereabouts. There are quite a few of them still working that experienced wars and the Great Depression. They value the work that they do and the contribution that they make and they know about sacrifice. They're very disciplined and loyal people who also very connected and influential in the workforce. So, don't discount them, and always be respectful and remember that you could probably learn something from them. I think you also should remember that with this generation, the women stayed in the home. They just didn't work. Of course, there are exceptions to every rule, but for the most part, women stayed in the home to raise the family and to run the household while the man went to work to earn a living.

Baby Boomers

Born between 1946 and 1964, they're going to range in age from 53 to 71. They used to be the largest percentage of workers in the workforce. Today, they are 44.6 million of the workforce. They grew up in the '60s during a time of great prosperity and economic growth. They experienced assassinations like the assassination of Martin Luther King, then they went through Watergate and the resignation of our president, Richard Nixon. You had highly educated women beginning to enter the workforce with the baby boomers, unlike the previous generation and equality of the sexes were very important to them. This is pretty much the first generation that you began to see dual-income families. Baby boomers are very work-centric or "Workaholics". They get up and start work early in the morning, and they work until late at night. They have a lot of respect for money.

Generation X

Born between 1965 and 1980, they range in age from 37 to 52. They represent 52.7 million of the workforce, and while that seems like that might be the most, it's not. They've just been overtaken by the millennials. They've experienced disappointment in leaders and therefore do not have a lot of respect for leaders of any kind, whether it be in the workforce, or political leaders. Even leaders of the church. They're very media savvy because they grew up with MTV. The Internet became an integral part of their lives, and they grew up with game boxes like Xbox and PlayStation. But they have a lot of anxiety about their health and their safety. They worry a lot about their jobs and the security of their jobs and their finances. They believe in "free agency" and they focus on the here and now. It's difficult to retain them in the workforce because they're very entrepreneurial by nature. They're big believers in work-life balance, and it's actually their number one preference. They want to make sure that they're measured by outcomes and not necessarily how many hours they work because they want to balance their life with their family as opposed to just working all the time.

Millennials or Gen Y

Sometimes you'll hear people call this group the echo boomers, and that's interesting because most people think that the millennials and the baby boomers are not at all alike or are opposites, and that's not true. They were born between 1981 and 1999. They range in ages from 18 to 36. They are the largest percentage of the workforce, and they continue to grow. They are now 53.5 million of the workforce. They were born into the computer and the digital era, and they were raised on heavy praise and self-esteem boosting curriculum. This is the generation of the participation awards and they feel very empowered and optimistic about everything. They will change jobs about every 1.3 years, and that's based on the Bureau of Labor and Statistics information. Thirty-seven percent were under or unemployed during the recession, according to Pew Research. They are very comfortable with diversity, which could be their strongest asset.

IGen or Generation Z

Born in 1996 and after, this generation is not quite in the workforce yet. They are considered the Super Connected generation because they do not remember a time before the internet. They grew up with cell phones and social media is the norm. The are less rebellious, more tolerant and completely unprepared for adulthood. They are the next generation to enter the workforce so we need to plan for their entry in much the same way as we have planned for the Millennials to enter the workforce.

The iGen or Generation Z will be entering the workforce soon, but for now, we will focus on the largest four work groups. Now that we know who they are, let's talk about the communications preferences for each group and recap what's important to them.

Traditionalists, or the older generation value loyalty and fair play. Ethics are first and foremost and they expect unconditional respect. They are big believers in giving back, they honor their commitments and they have the "whatever it takes" attitude. They believe in acknowledgment of both their own accomplishments and other people, and they also believe in "paying your dues."

Then, you have the baby boomers that are very process-oriented, and they play by the rules. They believe in rewards and money and are very materialistic. They're very work-centric, and some would even say "they live to work." They definitely like process and collaboration, and they flourish with coaching and mentoring.

Generation X, which are very results-oriented, work to live as opposed to live to work. They value the quality of their work-life balance and are very self-reliant. They grow with independent research, meaning they will work independently on research just to teach themselves. They believe they can learn from the boss, and the boss can also learn from them. This sometimes is referred to as the forgotten generation because so much attention is directed to baby boomer and now Millennials.

The Generation Y or millennials are very optimistic. They like to make a very quick impact. They seek out responsibility, but they also seek out feedback. They follow their passions and they believe in autonomy and flexibility, but they're masters at multitasking. They're very candid and express themselves openly, but they're very open to coaching and mentoring.

Now let's talk about work styles and technology. Email was, for the traditionalist and the boomers, just something else to learn, but not so much these days. Generation X feels like email is the best way to stay in touch, and Gen Y thinks that email is not nearly as good as instant messaging, blogging, and texting. Text messages are for techie kids, according to the traditionalists and boomers. Gen X just thinks that text messages are good for short, quick messages. And Gen Y'ers use it all day every day.

For traditionalists and boomers, PowerPoint is effective and professional. Gen Xers consider it their right arm, but Gen Y'ers think it's pretty boring in a speech, and it's hard to make it interesting. Face-to-face meetings are vital to a traditional and a boomer. Generation X thinks they're key, and Gen Y is uncomfortable. It feels confrontational and too formal to them.

Imagine the difficulty in bridging the gap for all of those different styles. When you're communicating with each of these generations, there are certain things you have to remember.

When you're communicating with traditionalists, they're private by nature, so don't expect them to share their thoughts. A face-to-face or written communication is preferred by the traditionalist, and don't let them feel their time is being wasted. Words are critical versus body language. Make sure that you use the right words with traditionalists.

When communicating with baby boomers, body language is very important. Face-to-face or written communication is very much preferred by baby boomers, and so is setting context and history. Also it is very important that they enjoy telling stories. Baby boomers speak directly and answer questions thoroughly with details, so they expect the same from you. They value tactfulness and seriousness, and they're likely to read procedural manuals cover-to-cover.

When communicating with Gen Xers, they use email primarily to communicate. They talk in short bites, and you need to talk in short bites to capture their attention. You need to ask for their feedback, and then give them feedback often. You need to share information and keep them in the loop, and use an informal, direct communication style.

When communicating with Generation Y, don't talk down to them. Use "just in time" communication and social networking like Email, blogging, Twitter, IM'ing, and text messaging, even Facebook. Ask for their feedback and give feedback to them often. Use humor and don't take yourself too seriously with these guys. Offer alternatives to manual and textbooks like online training with short snippets, maybe even video training. I would suggest putting it on YouTube for them. I love YouTube myself, but if you put it on YouTube and then create video training, you'll get their attention much more quickly.

Be clear and straightforward when delegating. Don't say things like, "you might want to consider" or "have you thought about." Don't be afraid to say, "I need you to." You should say, "I need you to complete task XYZ by a certain date." Be very specific, clear, and straightforward when delegating.

Think about this: A Generation Y member of your staff

consistently shows up for meetings late, and on occasion, they're late for work, too. He produces excellent work and has terrific interpersonal and technical skills.

How do you handle this? Are you upset at his lateness? If so, how do you address this? Do you consider generational differences when planning your conversations with him?

Is it the responsibility of the older or the younger generations to shift their style? See, I would suggest that it's all of the above. If you have been clear in setting expectations then you decision is made easier. Managing your communications and your expectations of all the different generations is important.

Think about managing your respective elders or those baby boomers and the traditionalists that are still working for you. You need to ask their opinions so that you understand their mind frame, and don't assume that there's a problem with the age gap because if you do that shows disrespect.

If you think they're slow or less productive or less technically savvy and you just assume that, then you insult them. You also need to remind yourself that they aren't your parents and you have to manage the challenges that they may make to your authority. But you should leverage their technical expertise and their institutional knowledge because they're walking around with a lot of experience, a lot of intellectual capital, a lot of knowledge.

If you learn what motivates them, things like security and recognition, then you can complement them. Don't compete with them, but complement them and offer them recognition when you notice things that they do that contribute, but delegate and seek their counsel.

The way to best communicate with them is face-to-face as that is likely their preferred method, and then show your appreciation for their contribution and the value that they're adding.

When you're managing your communication with Gen Y, you need to provide frequent, detailed feedback and accolades to them. Give them a team to work with. You need to designate shorter deadlines for these guys so that you keep their attention and keep them focused on that deadline. That way, you have more deadlines over a longer period of time, but they can celebrate those wins quickly. Teach them how to impact your workplace. Don't just assume they know.

Coach them on written and face-to-face communications so they can communicate up, down, and laterally. Then, feed their entrepreneurialism. Give them a task whose success is based on an outcome, and then don't micromanage them. Let them facilitate their lives outside of work.

How are we going to use this information? How are we going to pull it all together? Now that four generations and in many cases, five, are working together in offices around the country, how will workplace customs change when it comes to communication? See, the answers to this don't come easily, and existing research gives us a glimpse into how some common assumptions about different generations are just wrong. For instance, a recent Nielsen survey indicated that members of Generation X might actually be the happiest users of social media, not millennials or Generation Z.

Let's look past the assumptions and think about how the different generations could shape the workforce communication in the coming years. Just remember that generational groups or cohorts have different overarching values. Of course, members of the same generation will also have different beliefs from one another, but because generations come into their own during different historical moments, there are some criterion that seem to give each group some common, overarching values.

When you look at it that way, it's not surprising that people born before World War II tend to value loyalty quite highly. Those who were born into the economic boom that followed the war are typically highly optimistic and expect personal recognition. Members of Generation X experienced hands-off parenting and were the latchkey kids which seems to have led to self-reliance and skepticism in some.

Millennials experienced the consequences of 9/11 and the great recession as well as a more tightly networked world. They value connection, sincerity, and flexibility.

How do these differing values affect communication and teaming? Because of their valued backgrounds, members of different generations may value formal or informal approaches. Some will desire more or less praise, and some will have varying perspectives when it comes to divergent thinking and conformity.

We will need to put ourselves in somebody else's shoes. While you can't assume that you'll know what another person is feeling or what they think, trying to empathize with somebody from a different background could help you figure out what makes them tick and what motivates them. We've talked about this earlier in the book. Studies are starting to show that millennials want more feedback from their managers, and they want to receive it more frequently. They will likely need to be taught how to be a member of a team.

Most agree that millennials appreciate authenticity in their interactions with supervisors. That means opening up about successes, struggles, and failures. This could be challenging for managers from different generational backgrounds, but maintaining an approachable demeanor will become increasingly important. In certain situations, forthright communication can be more beneficial than a controlled message, and if you're uncomfortable, then I suggest that you give more feedback. Or, hire a coach for them and let them get that feedback from that coach if it's just too uncomfortable.

Just remember that each generation collaborates differently. Interestingly enough, millennials and traditionalists seem to have similar attitudes toward their current job. Isn't that funny? In a recent study, the overwhelming majority of both groups reported positive outlooks about their engagement at work and about their morale.

This could indicate that many organizations are ripe to reap the rewards of cross-generational collaboration, but how do you make sure that everybody feels included on the team? In a multi-generational environment, it's wise to mix and match strategies like the team building events favored by younger workers, and the opinion sharing practices promoted by their older counterparts.

Younger generations might feel more comfortable communicating their thoughts when they feel like they know their coworkers, while other generations might need a structured forum to weigh in on key decisions. Remember that technology is efficient, but face-to-face is ideal. Contrary to what we might assume, the majority of Millennials and Generation Z have reported a preference for in-person contact over IMs and emails.

While they value the ability of technological advancements in productivity to help them complete tasks, workers in the younger generations still see the value in human contact when it comes to teaming, collaboration and management. An effective communication strategy will take that into account. While a quick IM could be a good way to check in on a specific detail, a private, in-person setting is the best way to have a longer conversation.

To effectively work together, everybody, from Generation Z to experienced baby boomers, is going to have to understand each other's values. As I've said before, when we try to understand where individuals from different generations are coming from, we get a better sense of how best we can communicate our ideas to each other, express our opinions about how work performance can be improved, and share our thoughts in a more effective manner. The way we work together isn't the only thing we need to rethink.

CHAPTER SIX:

UNDERSTANDING HOW YOUR MIND WORKS SO YOU CAN UNDERSTAND OTHERS

People have different ways of communicating their experiences. Some express themselves in pictures (visual). Others talk about how things sound to them (auditory), and then others speak about how things feel (kinesthetic). We all have a certain mental syntax or order by which we process information. We can use this syntax to create a mental map.

A mental map is a powerful way of expressing thought patterns, pictures, and associations that already exist in the brain. When new information is matches existing knowledge, it's accepted. When it doesn't mesh with your preconceived ideas or your past experiences, it receives very little consideration, is distorted, or is just outright ignored.

Each of us have preferred modes of thinking and communicating. As we have discussed, **visual people, or visuals** "see" the world. They think by making pictures in their mind. They'll understand something better if they can actually see it, and their appearance is very important to them. There are some preferred words and phrases that they will use that will provide clues for you.

Bright	Bird's eye view	Catch a glimpse
Clar	Colorful	Clear
Colorful	Envisage	Flash
Hazy	Highlight	Horizon
Illustrate	In light of	Look
Make a scene	Notice	Observe
Perceive	Perspective	Picture
Preview	Reflect	See
See eye-to-eye	Show	Tunnel vision
View	Watch	

People that have a visual primary modality will have specific characteristics. They will maintain good eye contact and will have good visual memory. Their voice will be high-pitched and fast. Most visuals will be good with directions.

Auditories "hear" the world. They think by analyzing sounds. They get more information from how you say things than from what you're actually saying. They love to hear themselves and others talk. You'll hear them saying, I'm just thinking out loud. People with a primarily auditory modalities will also have preferred words that you can listen for.

Accent	Articulate	Ask
Call on	Discuss	Express
Harmony	Hear	Inquire
Loud	Listen	Mention
Noisy	Oral	Outspoken
Quiet	Pronounce	Remark
Resonate	Ring	Ring a bell
Say	Scream	Sound
Speak	Static	Talk
Tell	Tone	

Characteristics of a person with a primary modality of auditory will have a lower-pitched voice that is rhythmic and smooth. They will try to sound good and may talk to themselves. They like concerts and music.

Lastly, the kinesthetics "feel" the world. They act on what they feel. They get more information from touch, emotions, gut instincts, and hunches. They love to touch people and things. Just like the other two modalities, kinesthetics has preferred words that will let you know their preference.

Affect	Boils down to	Burning
Clumsy	Concern	Dull
Euphoric	Feel	Firm
Grab	Grasp	Handle
Hard	Hit	Impress
Intuit	Know	Pressure
Relax	Rough	Rub
Rush	Slipped my mind	Smooth
Stress	Suffer	Tackle
Touch	Warm	

They will feel hot or cold about you and they like to touch people and things. When speaking, there will be frequent pauses in the conversation while they determine how they feel about a certain topic.

Each of us also has a distinct personality style that was likely set in stone by age five or six. These styles do not change much as we grow and mature but we can learn to adapt our personality styles to others to be more effective.

There are a number of personality assessment tools available and each of them describe our personality types using different vernacular or terms. The outcome is similar and the benefit of knowing your style is not dependent on which assessment you use. I prefer the DiSC personality profile so I will use that reference point when talking about the different personality styles.

There are basically four primary styles with 3 variations of each style. The styles tell us what our natural or organic personality style is and how we interact with people of differing styles. This know allows you to understand yourself better and then using that knowledge to adapt your style to someone else's style.

The first style is called **Dominance or Director** and a person with this style is interested in getting immediate results, taking action and challenging themselves and others. They are motivated by power and authority, competition, winning and success. You will notice self-confidence, directness, forcefulness and risk-taking. This personality style fears a loss of control, being taken advantage of and vulnerability. They may seem to have a lack of concern for others, to be impatient and insensitive.

Secondly, there is the **Conscientiousness** style. A person with this style prioritizes ensuring accuracy, maintaining stability and challenging assumptions. They will be motivated by opportunities to use their expertise, gain knowledge and an attention to detail. You will notice precision, analysis, skepticism, reserve and quiet about them. The Conscientiousness style fears criticism, slipshod methods and being wrong. They may see overly critical, have a tendency to overanalyze and they may isolate themselves.

The third style is **Steadiness** and a person with this style will be supportive, maintain stability and enjoy collaboration. They are motivated by stable environments, sincere appreciation, cooperation and opportunities to help. You will notice they have patience, are team players, have a calm approach, are a good listener and have humility. A Steadiness personality style will fear a loss of stability, change, loss of harmony and offending others. They may be overly accommodating, have a tendency to avoid change and be indecisive.

And last but certainly not least are the **Influence** personality style that prioritizes expressing enthusiasm, taking action and encouraging collaboration. They are motivated by social recognition, group activities and friendly relationships. You will notice that they are charming, enthusiastic, sociable, optimistic and talkative. They will fear social rejection, disapproval, loss of influence and being ignored. They may seem impulsive, disorganized and have a lack of follow-through.

Now that we have an idea of some of the characteristics and personality styles that people may have, how do we determine what personality style we and others are? When trying to elicit these characteristics, we need to ask open-ended questions. Ask an open-ended question, then be quiet and note the exact words that the other person uses. When a person answers an open-ended question, he stops focusing outward and goes inside his mind. At that instant, he becomes relatively unaware of the words he's going to use.

These words are going to point back in time to meaningful memories and emotional experiences. So, just listen. Most people will tell you more about themselves than they think. If you take note of the particular words they use you can tell by which of the three basic methods of perceiving the world they use which one is their primary modality.

We're going to discuss the techniques and how you use them later in the chapter when we discuss perceptions and accessing clues. When you ask them an open-ended question, you'll be able to tell if you watch their eye movements and their body movements whether they are visual, auditory, or kinesthetic.

You can then determine which personality style they may be by paying attention to the way they conduct themselves. Use the above descriptions to get as close as you can to what you think their personality style is. You can also contact our office and we can help you with the assessments and educating your team about the different styles.

These observations are very important to building a diverse team. It is human nature to draw people that are "like" you to your teams and many times a team ends up not being very diverse because of this. These tools will help you make sure that you have a diverse team from a personality and modality perspective.

"The state of your life is nothing more than a reflection of your state of mind." – Wayne W. Dyer

"We are constantly bombarded with so much sensory information that it is impossible for us to pay attention to everything," says Sandra Blakeslee, an award-winning science writer for the New York Times. "Our subconscious mind scans our environment and selects what it deems may be important for us to notice. Even then, people not only see things the way they are, they also tend to see what they expect to see, as well as what they want to see. Much of human perception is based not on information flowing into the brain from the outside world but what the brain, based on previous experience, expects to happen next."

I have outlined some tools in this chapter that you can use to determine how to work with and communicate with others. It is my desire that you will use these tools to help in building a well-rounded, high performing team.

It's important that you understand these tools so that when you're communicating with someone or interacting for the first time with someone, you can read their body language. Ask them open-ended questions so that you can figure out what their communication style is, and then begin to mirror and match them to build rapport and a solid foundation for a relationship.

If you begin to mirror and match them using their preferred words it will help them get a better understanding of what you are trying to say. If you have an agenda that you'd like to move forward or you're working on a project with someone and you need to get them to buy into your idea or simply support you in the project. Communicating in their style is very important. It's just as important as the multi-generational communication styles that we talked about in chapter five.

CHAPTER SEVEN:

BUILDING A HIGH PERFORMING TEAM

"The strength of the team is each individual member. The strength of each member is the team." Phil Jackson

High performing teams are rare and at a premium whether it is a sports team or a team within a company. To be successful as a team leader you have to focus on the success of the team rather than individual performance. A team is highly focused on their goals and together achieve superior business results.

Have you ever contributed to a high performing team? If so, what did the team look like?

I had the great honor and pleasure to lead one of the best high performing teams within one of the largest software companies in the world. We were all focused on the success of the team and there were no egos to get in the way of that. From that success, I learned how to build a strong team and so I will attempt to share my learnings with you here.

What makes a team successful enough to be called "high performing"? How do you make sure that everyone is focused on the same things? Is it possible to keep team cohesiveness even when there is conflict? Can you build the level of trust that is required to operate at such a high level on a diverse team? These are the questions that we attempt to answer in this chapter.

All high performing teams seem to have the same components in common and so let's discuss each one of them to give you a good understanding of what is involved.

Attract the Right Team Members
The first thing that is to figure out the team's purpose. Once you have determined this you can assemble the group's members. You may have inherited a group or "team" due to an organizations structure or you may have to attract and build a team from scratch. We are going to address building one from scratch in this book.

As a leader, you need to learn how to identify and attract talent. Use the tools we have discussed in this book and also look for tools from other sources as well. Teams will perform better if you chose the right talent. Organizations that put a lot of resources into identifying and recruiting talent do better.

Remember that you need a well-rounded and diverse team. This means diversity in ethnicity, diversity in experience, diversity of skills and diversity of personality styles. When attracting talent you will need to make a concerted effort to attract a diverse group with different strengths in order to perform at the highest levels.

Define the Structure of the Team
You will need to create and define the structure of the team. This will require that you determine the team members' roles. If you think of a sports team, everyone has their position to play and

success happens when each player is playing their role effectively. In addition, it should be made clear what the interdependencies are for the team members. Real teams are interdependent so that they rely on one another to get the job done! These interdependencies should be understood by the team members so that each person understands how their role impacts the success of the team.

High performing teams have a clear structure that is communicated to all members of the team. There is no confusion about who is to do what and how those roles and tasks are to interact with each other.

Create an Operational Agreement
What is an operational agreement? It can be whatever you want it to be. The principles can be similar to core values but with one important caveat; they are behavioral, tactical guides. They should provide direction to the team so that there is no ambiguity.

Set up a meeting this is specifically to address establishing the operational agreement for the team. Make sure that you are prepared for a productive and uninterrupted time. Give the team members some examples of what you will need to accomplish before the meeting. This will give them time to think about it and come to the meeting ready to offer ideas and prepared to defend and/or advocate for the ideas they deem important.

As the leader of the group, it will be your job to facilitate the conversation and NOT TO set the principles. While you may have certain behaviors that you will encourage and expect, you do not want these principles to be perceived as directives from you. You can make suggestions and then let others put their ideas on the table first.

Once this brainstorming is complete and you have a list of

ideas, have the team rank their 3-5 top operational ideas. Create a neutral way to them to vote on the top ideas so you can narrow them down to 3 – 5 core principles. How you do it is less important than the result. The key is that having no more than five final principles is important.

There will need to be shared **accountability** amongst the team. This is where the process can either thrive or break down into a frustrating waste of time. Keep the team engaged in a discussion about how these principles will be maintained. Will the group call each other out on them? Or, will an audit be conducted at the end of a monthly meeting? There needs to be agreement on how the team will keep and hold each other accountable and they need to be the ones to come up with this agreement.

Finally, create a way to keep the operating agreement visible to all team members. Post them before team meetings and/or create framed graphics that can sit on desks. Whatever it takes to keep them visible, do it!

You will also need to provide clear and constant feedback so create a **communications plan**. A system should be in place so that team members receive ongoing feedback while doing their jobs. Teams need to know how they are doing in order to stay motivated and correct performance problems or inefficiencies. A system should be in place to allow for team members to receive ongoing feedback while a part of the team and doing their job.

Determine how the team will handle **decision-making**. Whether you, as the leader, makes all the decisions or they are made by a consensus process, the team needs to understand beforehand how decisions will be made. The team can make decisions when there is natural agreement. In the cases where there is some disagreement, the decision can be made by the team lead or executive sponsor. This will reduce conflict when a decision or choice has to be made.

A very important agreement is how **conflict resolution** will be handled. Disagreement should be viewed as a good thing and conflicts should be managed properly. Make sure that criticism is constructive and is oriented toward problem solving and removing obstacles. The team needs to engage in extensive discussion and make sure that every member gets a change to contribute, even the introverts. Document the decisions and make this a part of the overall operational agreement.

In the event that there is the need for escalation, then you need to have clearly communicated the **escalation path**. This can take a simple hierarchical form or org chart that clearly communicates the different levels of escalation if resolution of the issue has not occurred.

There should be agreement that allows team members to **challenge the status quo**. If innovation is important, it is critical that team members feel secure in being able to challenge processes. If they feel improvements can be made then they should feel free to openly communicate their ideas. Teams need to be open to considering and constructively criticize existing practices when needed.

Performance Goals
Every effective team has members with individual and unique roles within the team. It is expected that they will execute flawlessly within their role. As the team lead, you will need to distribute individual tasks among the team members and use the agreed upon accountability system to hold them accountable. Each team member needs to carry his or her own weight. They also need to respect the team processes and other members.

One Set of Goals
Teams need to be focused on shared goals and outcomes. Commitment to this set of goals is essential to the success of the

team. If developed well, team goals should allow both the team as a unit and the individual members to achieve both personal and group goals. This will ensure that everyone is working toward the same goals.

Maintain Stability and Trust

Once you have gathered the team and have established the operational agreement, now you need to maintain stability, build and maintain trust on the team. It takes a lot of time for team members to learn to work together at an optimum level and this is especially true in complex tasks. You can use a team-based reward system to incentivize and motivate the team. I discourage using or placing too much emphasis on individual rewards as this can lead to in-fighting and resentment. A combination of team and individual based rewards is best.

Encourage and create a learning environment and emphasize the development of the team. Make sure they are learning through successes but especially through mistakes. A team that has an attitude of continuous improvement and where members are motivated to develop their skills and knowledge are high performing teams.

Focus on the Collective Mission

Mission driven teams and organizations perform better because they are all pulling in the same direction. They see beyond their individual workload and tasks and feel they are working for a higher purpose. It is essential to the success of the team that team members be committed to the shared mission, or they should be replaced.

All of these rules apply whether a team is self-governing or whether they have a formal appointed leader. The key is to put the time and energy into adhering to these best practices. When people have deep trust in each other and in the team's purpose, they feel free to express their feelings and ideas. Team members are clear on how to work together and how accomplish tasks. Everyone understand both the team and individual goals. They all know what is expected. Team members will self-govern and will actively diffuse tension and friction because the atmosphere is more relaxed and informal.

While the leadership of the team may shift periodically, as appropriate, to drive the desired results, no individual members are more important than the team. Having an operating agreement provides a path for collaborative success by providing clarity that builds trust and accountability. You will be able to unlock the value of the team members by empowering them to contribute. Job satisfaction improves, the team members stay engaged in their work and it is a win, win, win.

CHAPTER EIGHT:

DEFINING YOUR LEADERSHIP SKILLS

"Leadership is the art of getting someone else to do something you want done because he wants to do it." – Dwight D. Eisenhower

"A leader is best when people barely know he exists. When his work is done, they will say: we did it ourselves." – Lao Tzu

RJ House, in The GLOBE Study of Culture, Leadership, and Organizations: 2004 defines "leadership" organizationally and narrowly as "the ability of an individual to influence, motivate, and enable others to contribute toward the effectiveness and success of the organizations of which they are members." Based on this you could say that leadership is influencing people to get things done to a standard and quality above their norm. And doing it willingly.

As a part of a team interaction, leadership is a complex activity involving influencers and participants who are both leaders and followers. It also includes a multitude of possible outcomes; the achievement of goals, the commitment of individuals to those goals, the enhancement of group cohesion and the reinforcement of change of the organizational structure. We will talk about change management in the next chapter.

The *role* of a leader is to create followers. In order to create followers you have to incorporate the skills outlined earlier in this book by developing the trust and understanding of the team. A leader's *task* is to bring about constructive and necessary change. This requires confidence in the process and support of management. The *responsibility* of a leader is to bring about that change in a way that is responsive to the true and long-term needs of all team members. The greatest *source of power* available to a leader is the trust that derives from faithfully serving followers. This means that you need to become a servant leader and put the team ahead of the personal or individual.

Leadership attributes include a variety of characteristics such as values, character, motives, habits, traits, style, behaviors, and skills. The key is to understand all of these things about yourself. Do you have a good understanding of you values? Are you motives pure with only the team's interest at heart? Are you habits those of a strong leader that is worthy of following?

We have talked about personality styles and behavior in previous chapters. So we will discuss the soft skills that will compliment your styles and modalities to ensure you are perceived as a strong leader that people want to follow.

Effective leaders recognize that they still have a lot to learn and that what they know is very little in comparison. To be better at pursuing and achieving objectives, you should be open to new ideas, insights, and revelations that can lead to better ways to accomplishing your goals. This continuous learning process can be exercised by engaging yourself in a constant dialogue with your peers, advisers, consultants, team members, suppliers, customers, and competitors. In other words, remember that you can learn something from everyone that you meet no matter their position.

Leading others is not simply a matter of style or following some how-to guides or recipes. Ineffectiveness of leaders seldom results from a lack of know-how or how-to, nor is it typically due to inadequate managerial skills. It is about creating conditions under which all your followers can perform independently and effectively toward a common objective. It all boils down to your attitude toward others and your willingness to commit to continuous improvement.

We will take a values-based leadership approach here that is not only fair and just but also highly effective in today's complex organizations. It is based on a variety of skills that start with your ideas and values. You will need an understanding of the differing and conflicting needs of your followers.

Your success will depend on your ability to energize followers to pursue a better goal than they had thought possible. That means that you first must believe it yourself. Then you need to communicate clearly to the team. You will need to use your skills in creating a values-based umbrella large enough to accommodate the various interests of followers, but keep it focused enough to direct all their energies in pursuit of a common goal.

Developing a clear Vision is one of the keys to leadership and promotion. The one quality that all leaders have in common is that they have a clear and exciting vision for the future. This is something that only the leader can do. Only the leader can **think about** the future and **plan for** the future each day. Leaders have the ability to communicate this vision in such a way that others "buy in" and eventually see the vision as belonging to them.

I am constantly trying to "model" visionary leaders and I encourage you to do the same. You can accelerate your ability in this area simply by modeling what others have done. While you may not always be able to speak to them directly to create their internal strategy, you can read about the actions and strategy they are implementing and learn from that. Following are some examples of the visionary leaders from a variety of areas because we can learn from all of them.

Nitin Nohria, Dean of Harvard Business School wrote about Lee Iacocca:

"Our fascination with the CEO as a celebrity leader dates back to Lee Iacocca. He captured the moment because he saw and seized on a series of secular changes that crept up almost unnoticeably.

By the early 1970s, the major U.S. carmakers seemed unassailable. Then came the OPEC oil embargo and the energy crisis that followed. Many people thought that the oil shock was just a temporary, macro interruption. But this geopolitical event revealed a larger set of coalescing forces that allowed the Japanese carmakers to erode Detroit's dominance. By 1980, Japan had become the world's largest automobile producer and all of the major U.S. automobile companies lost money. The biggest loser of all was Chrysler, which posted a record loss of $1.7 billion.

Then comes this larger-than-life figure, Iacocca. He was the first modern leader to use the force of his persona to turn around an American icon. Iacocca pledged that he would take an annual salary of $1 until he returned Chrysler to profitability. He persuaded the government to authorize a $1.5 billion loan guarantee using taxpayers' dollars. But he knew he couldn't keep going back to that well. And so Iacocca seized on three forces that were reshaping the American business landscape and yoked them to his advantage.

First, there was technology. Iacocca understood that the

Japanese threat stemmed from a fundamentally more productive way of managing manufacturing, which he'd have to mimic. Then came labor. Iacocca was among the first to recognize that there needed to be a more cooperative compact between labor and management. Under his leadership, Chrysler was the first American corporation to put members of the United Auto Workers on its board. And finally, Iacocca leveraged America's radically changing demographics. His genius was to see that the baby boomers were starting families, so he bet Chrysler's future on the minivan. Ultimately, Iacocca succeeded at turning around Chrysler because he acted on all three fronts simultaneously.

Some say that we've developed a dangerous infatuation with charismatic leaders. And they're right. But that doesn't mean we were wrong to believe in these people in the first place. You can't put your faith in the institution when it's crumbling. You don't trust Chrysler. But you do trust Iacocca."

A vision of what can be, arouses emotion and motivates people to give their best. The most powerful vision is always qualitative, aimed at, and described in terms of values and mission rather than quantitative, which is described in terms of money and numbers. You also must be a good communicator in order to get your vision out to the team and to get complete buy in to your ideas.

A Disney VP of technology, Nikki Katz has a degree from Stanford and a résumé with experience at companies such as Yahoo. She also had a big vision based on something she is passionate about; giving women access to technical skills training and the jobs that go with it. Women can join Disney's software-engineering workforce in a most unconventional way. They become participants in CODE: Rosie, a program that gives women already at the company in non-technical roles an opportunity to switch careers.

The participants will begin class, with MacBooks and welcome packets already in place on rows of desks. After three months of training—in everything from basic computer-science concepts to programming languages such as Python—they'll segue into a yearlong apprenticeship consisting of two six-month chunks in different teams within the company. Then they'll have the opportunity to take a job within one of Disney's technical groups.

Nikki Katz had a vision that became a reality because she was able to gain support of her vision. She utilized her education, skills, and passion to convince Disney of the need to integrate this program. The first cohort of women have successfully completed the course and are in their "apprenticeship jobs" and the second cohort of women are getting ready to start the program! Just another example of a visionary leader and the benefits that are being realized by the women of Disney but also by Disney itself!

Having a vision as the leader of a team and being able to motivate the team to act on that vision, is integral to the overall success of the team. The leader of the team is solely responsible for getting "buy-in" to the vision from the members of the team.

A study at Stanford Business School examined the qualities that companies look for in promoting young managers toward senior executive positions. The study concluded that one of the most important qualities required for great success was the ability to put together a team and then function as part of that team. Since teams ultimately do all the work, and the managers' output is the output of the team, the ability to select team members, set objectives, delegate responsibility and get the job done, was central to success in management.

Another key to leadership success is to "keep your cool." You must be able to operate well under pressure, especially in a crisis. Keeping your cool during a crisis means practicing patience and self-control under difficult or disappointing circumstances. You should never, ever, speak of your frustrations with direct reports! At all times, even when you are at your most disappointed, you must, at least publicly, toe the company line.

In today's market and corporate climate, it is becoming increasingly more important to find someone outside the company to run ideas by and to "vent" frustrations with. This alone could save your career or, more importantly, save your life (by reducing your stress levels). I highly recommend getting a Business or Executive Coach for this, simply because anything you discuss is confidential and it gives you an outlet to clear and eliminate limiting emotions.

The character and quality of a leader are often demonstrated in these critical moments under fire, when everyone is watching, observing, and privately taking notes. As Rudyard Kipling once said, "If you can keep your head when all around you are losing theirs and blaming it on you, then the world is yours and all that's in it." Your job as a leader is to have a clear vision of where you want to go and then to keep your cool when things go wrong, as they surely will.

Leadership is imperative for molding a group of people into a team, shaping them into a force that serves as a competitive business advantage. Leaders know how to make people function in a collaborative fashion, and how to motivate them to excel in their performance. Leaders also know how to balance the individual team member's quests with the goal of producing synergy - an outcome that exceeds the sum of individual inputs. Leaders require their team members to blend the quest for personal best in concert with the team effort.

Leaders also help each of their team members or followers to develop into an effective self-leader by providing them with the behavioral and cognitive skills necessary to exercise self-leadership. They establish values, model, encourage, reward, and in many other ways foster self-leadership in individuals, teams, and wider organizational cultures.

Running the mighty GE enterprise, with its twelve major businesses, Jack Welch didn't seem like a traditional manager. He seemed more like a super-leader: "I have no idea how to produce a good TV program and just as little about how to build an engine...My job is to chose the best people and to provide them with dollars. That's how the game is played." Jack Welch abandoned the old practice of setting goals for GE's business leaders. "Now, we don't reward them according to whether or not they reach their objectives. They're all going to get paid on their improvement, and they know that. In bureaucratic companies, they waste a lot of time on making budgets. They waste energy. The world is changing quickly. We can't afford to waste time in bureaucracy. GE is an informal company. We trust each other." (Jack Welch quoted in Nikkei Business, February 21, 1994)

An important measure of a leader's own success is the success of his or her followers. The strength of a leader is measured by the ability to facilitate the self-leadership of others. The first critical step towards this goal is to master self-leadership. If leaders want to lead somebody, they must first lead themselves.

CHAPTER NINE:

BE THE CHANGE EXPERT

"Leaders disrupt. Managers Stabilize" – The Leadership Freak

To build, grow, motivate and operate a high performing team, a leader must be able to implement change. There is a right way and a wrong way to push for organizational change. One of the most important things to remember is that you need to communicate clearly and frequently. Keeping the team informed and making sure that they understand the change and why you are making the change, is critical to successfully implementing it.

Are you considering implementing the team building tools in this book or others that may be new. Is this a serious change effort in your organization? Address these concerns, in this order, so you can get everyone on board and moving in the right direction.

People don't want to be told about the change is or that it is good until they understand it. You should **share information** as plainly and as completely as possible. In the absence of clear, factual communication, people tend to create their own information about the change, and rumors become facts.

Leaders should prepare to **answer questions** such as: What is the change? Why is it needed? What's wrong with the way things are now? How much and how fast does the organization need to change? The answers to these and all questions need to be answered without defensiveness or judgement. People process change in different ways. Some will process the information and embrace the change more quickly than others. Don't judge regardless of how they process. Your job is to ensure that they process the information and understand it completely. Most importantly, they need to feel like you heard them!

Once information concerns are satisfied, people will want to know **how the change will affect them personally**. The following questions are common, and may not always be expressed openly: What's in it for me to change? Will I win or lose? Will I look good? How will I find the time to implement this change? Will I have to learn new skills? Can I do it?

People always want to know how the change will play out for them. They wonder if they have the skills and resources to implement the change. It's important to remember that as the organization changes people may think their current commitments are being threatened. It's normal for people to focus on what they are going to lose before they consider what they might gain.

These personal concerns have to be surfaced and addressed. Otherwise, as Werner Erhard has often said, "What you resist, persists." If you don't permit people to deal with their feelings about what's happening, those feelings stay around. Have you ever said to yourself, "I'm glad I got that off my chest?" If so, you know the relief that comes from sharing your concerns openly. The good news is that when people share them openly, their concerns often dissipate.

If you address the first two concerns effectively, people will be ready to hear information on the details involved in implementing the change. At this stage, they will be interested to hear how the thinking behind the change has been tested. They will also want to know where to go for technical assistance and solutions to problems that might arise.

You and your leadership team (if you have one) should be prepared to answer questions such as: What do I do first, second, third? How do I manage all the details? What happens if it doesn't work as planned? Where do I go for help? How long will this take? Is what we are experiencing typical? How will the organizational structure and systems change?

Once these implementation questions are answered, people tend to raise impact concerns. They may ask: Is the effort worth it? Is the change making a difference? Are we making progress? Are things getting better?

With the focus on evaluation, people with impact concerns are interested in the change's relevance and payoff. The good news is that if leaders have done a good job up to this point, this is the stage where people will sell themselves on the benefits of the change based on the answers to their questions and the relative merits of the results to be achieved.

Be prepared to share early wins and proof that the change is making a positive difference. If the change does not positively impact results–or people don't know how to measure success–it will be more difficult to keep the change initiative moving forward.

With some evidence that the change is moving the team in the right direction, momentum starts to build. Now you can look forward to questions and ideas focused on coordination and cooperation with others. Now you have a core group of people in the company that want to get everyone on board because they are convinced the change is making a difference.

Now you are at the stage where leaders can look forward to questions such as: Who else should be involved? How can we work with others to get them involved in what we are doing? How do we spread the word?

Once a change effort is well on its way toward complete adoption, you can expect to hear others begin asking about how the change can be refined. For example: How can we improve on our original idea? How do we make the change even better?

These type of refinement questions are a good sign and show that the people in the organization are focused on continuous improvement.

During any organizational change, some learnings usually occur. Take advantage of new opportunities for organizational improvement that often come to the surface at this stage. This requires that you pay attention and continue to listen to your team members so that you easily spot these new opportunities.

Take time with your next change initiative and if you do it right, you can drastically increase your chances of success. If you rush through the early stages, you might find yourself derailed as many of these concerns surface later in the project. This will kill momentum when it is needed most.

You've probably heard this before, but it's worth repeating here: People who help to plan the battle rarely battle the plan. While dealing with people's concerns about change may seem like a lot of hand-holding, it's important for you to remember that they too had to process information and personal concerns before they were ready to discuss impact and implementation.

CHAPTER TEN:

INTO ACTION:
INTEGRATING THE SKILLS

We started the book out by talking about our communications skills and then the same topic has been woven throughout the book. That just reiterates the importance of good communications skills in whatever we do and especially when building a team.

Rapport is also a big part of getting people to join your team and to establish the beginnings of a relationship. There are a number of ways to establish deep rapport and I encourage you to get really good at this skill. You can practice in your daily life by building rapport with people you interact with each day. Try using it with the wait staff the next time you go out to eat!

Once you have established rapport with someone then you can take the relationship to a deeper level by establishing trust. As we do this, we are able to influence each other and the relationship takes on a give and take that was not present before.

Remember that your body language and non-verbal communication are out front and public. Even without speaking a word we are communicating with our team members. Our attitude is infectious and speaks volumes about us. We can use out tone of voice to indicate our state of mind or mood. If you are in a less than positive state or frame of mind, you can change it immediately with your physiology.

The key is that you are congruent in what you are saying with your words, body language and non-verbal communications. For instance, if you are saying that you like something and yet you are rolling your eyes, your team will not believe that you mean that!

We also talked about listening skills and how important it is that you practice these skills to ensure the accuracy of what you heard. It is equally important to use your good listening skills to indicate that you are really interested in what your team member has to say.

Here are some tips to help you be a better listener:

Try avoid thinking that you know the answer or that you already know what the speaker wants to say before they actually finish what they are saying. By interrupting the speaker before letting them finish, you're essentially saying that you don't value what they are saying. Try waiting 3 seconds after someone stops talking before you speak.

Many of us think we are trying to be helpful and while it may seem beneficial, it interferes with listening. It interferes because the listener is thinking about how to solve what he perceives to be the speaker's problem and he misses what the speaker is actually saying. Give your whole attention to whatever you're doing. It is worth emphasizing that the goal of good listening is simply to listen -- nothing more and nothing less. Trying to be helpful while listening also implies that you've made certain judgments about the speaker and can sometimes mean that the listener doesn't have complete respect for the speaker.

Some people feel that agreeing with the speaker during a heated discussion is a sign of weakness and they feel like they have to challenge every point the speaker makes. They do this even if they inwardly agree. The discussion then becomes a contest, with a score being kept for who wins the most points by arguing. Treating discussion as competition is one of the most serious barriers to good listening.

Good listening depends on listening just for the sake of listening without any ulterior motives. For instance, if you are trying to impress or to influence the speaker it will diminish your effectiveness as a listener. You will will not be able to pay complete attention while listening if you are busy trying to influence or impress the speaker.

Red flag words can provoke a reaction in the listener that wasn't necessarily what the speaker intended. When that happens, the listener won't be able to hear or pay full attention to what the speaker is saying. These words can trigger an unexpectedly strong association in the listener's mind, often due to the listener's beliefs or past experiences.

Sometimes people pay such close attention to detail, that they miss the overall meaning or context of a situation. Have you ever heard the saying "you can't see the forest for the trees"? Learn to use both the forest and the trees when offering explanations. The big picture "forest" provides context and meaning and the "trees" provides the specifics.

People have different styles of organizing thoughts when explaining complex situations. Some people tend to pay more attention to how things are different and we could call these people the difference people. Other people tend to look for how things are alike and we could call these people matchers.

If the speaker and listener are on opposite sides of the difference-matchers spectrum, the different mental styles can cause confusion or lack of understanding. It's important to achieve a good balance between difference (critical thinking) and matcher (metaphorical thinking). Even more important is for the listener to recognize when the speaker is using difference and when she is matching.

Often more than one of these issues can be present at once. For example, a speaker might be an over-difference user who has trouble seeing the forest, while the listener is an over-matcher who can see only the forest and never the trees. Those two will have even more trouble communicating if one or both has the habit of knowing the answer or treating all discussion as competition.

Good listening is arguably one of the most important skills to have in today's complex world of teaming. Corporate employees need it to solve complex problems quickly and stay competitive. Much can be gained by improving listening skills.

Another tool in your toolkit is building and maintaining relationships. This starts with your relationship with yourself so make sure you are clear about how you want that relationship to be. You should learn to balance give and receiving in any and all relationships and show your appreciation to those that you do have a relationship with.

Relationship building, influencing and motivating people are critical to the success of building a team. We are ALL in the people business no matter what our business is.

Only when we know what we believe ourselves can we influence ourselves and others. This quote has been one of my favorites for a long time. "If you believe in nothing, you will fall for anything." Have the strength of your convictions and you will win the respect of others.

As you build your team remember to make sure that you keep

diversity in mind. You will need a variety of thoughts, skills and knowledge to be successful. The need for diversity of thought and experience grows more and more important as the complexity of the corporate environment increases. Be aware that we are all influenced by unconscious biases and don't let yours get in the way of building a high performing team!

Keep in mind that you will also want to make sure the you have a good mix of personality styles and modalities to create a team that models a global perspective. It will help you to develop strategies that will assist you in communicating and working across this diverse team.

If you use the process outlined in Chapter Seven to build your team, you will have fewer bumps in the road. As clear communications increase the engagement of the team also increases.

I encourage my clients to continually and constantly improve their leadership skill. Just like everything else, leadership philosophy and trends mature and change over time. You must stay current with leadership and business trends to remain relevant.

Integration and Success

We have discussed an awful lot in this book, and it probably seems like a lot to take in. But I am convinced that if you can master the principles in this book, you will take your team further than you ever expected.   It is hard work and not for the faint of heart, but it is worth the effort.

I encourage you to master individual skills one at a time; then move on to the next skill. This can take as little as one week and up to 6 weeks. Once you have done that, you will be on your way to a successful and satisfying career of building an expert team leader and builder.

All of this can be accomplished while ensuring that you are not "stepping" on anyone along the way. If you focus on constant and continual education and improvement, your business relationships will become richer, deeper, and more rewarding. The benefit of doing such hard work is that your career will naturally follow in an upward curve and people will want to be on your teams.

I challenge you to take the next steps and to work on leadership skills. You will be pleasantly surprised how much more power and influence you will have in every area of your life.

Appendix A

Nonverbal Gestures That Indicate:
Openness, confidence:
- open hands, palms up
- unbuttoning or removing jacket (men)
- eye contact
- smile, leaning forward, relaxed
- hands away from the face, possibly behind back
- standing straight, feet slightly apart, shoulders squared
- hand in belt, thumb hooked in the waist
- clucking
- snapping fingers
- smacking palm

Cooperation, readiness:
- standing with hands on hips, feet apart, head tilted
- uncrossed legs
- a person moves closer to another
- unbuttoned coat (men)
- head cocked, finger to face, blinking or squinting
- welcoming handshake
- open arms or hands (palms out)
- smile
- eye contact
- rubbing palms together indicating an expectation of something pleasant
- hand to the chest in a man indicates loyalty (but in a woman it is defensiveness)
- touching, patting, holding hands to give reassurance

Professional:
- taking notes
- judgment gestures, especially hand to face
- leaning forward
- use of space in seating so as to avoid barriers
- eye contact
- Lincolnesque position

- absence of gestures indicative of dominance, indifference, defensiveness, etc. Take note of gestures signifying a desire to interrupt: ``school'' gesture of raising hand, tugging the ear, or just raising hand from table and then dropping back
- index finger to lip to restrain from interrupting
- hand on the arm of the speaker

Indifference, boredom:
- leg over the arm of the chair
- rhythmic drumming, tapping
- legs crossed
- shaking one foot (women)
- straighten up then slouch
- ``cold shoulder,'' turning away especially toward exit
- glancing at exit
- rigid, unmoving posture with fixed stare
- yawning
- hand holding up face, drooping eyelids
- fidgeting or rocking
- turning up nose and/or ``tsk'' sound (signifying disgust)

Evaluation, interest:
- hand to cheek gesture in the style of Rodin's *The Thinker* statue
- slight blinking or squinting
- chin stroking
- hands touching face especially upper lip
- leaning forward (positive) and leaning back (negative)
- head tilted, ear cocked
- peering over the top of glasses
- sucking on the tip of pencil or earpiece of glasses indicates a wish for nourishment in the form of more information
- arched eyebrows
- licking lips
- wrinkling nose
- scratching head
- ruffling hair

Doubt:
- pacing
- hand over nose
- eyes closed
- brow furrowed
- arched eyebrows
- frown
- scratching in front of ear
- rubbing eyes
- hand to face gestures (evaluative)
- pacing with head down and hands behind back or just standing—unwise to interrupt a person thus engaged
- scratching head
- pinching bridge of nose, especially with head lowered

Suspicion, secretiveness:
- folded arms, moving away from another
- crossed legs
- head tilted forward
- rubbing nose
- lack of eye contact
- hand covering mouth
- scratching in front of ear
- frown
- scrunching in with head down
- stolen look, sideways glance
- sideways positioning
- "poker face"
- deception indicated by lack of eye contact
- anxiety gestures
- looking at floor
- frequent swallowing
- wetting lips
- throat clearing
- scratching head

Need for reassurance:
- clenched hands with thumbs rubbing

- stroking arms
- cuticle picking
- hand pinching, sucking on pen, glasses, etc.
- touching chair before sitting
- hand to throat (women) often displaced to seemingly checking to see if necklace is still there

Anxiety:
- nail biting
- finger movement
- sighing
- hand wringing
- rapid, twitchy movements
- clearing throat
- tremors, especially knees
- heavy breathing
- voice strained
- lips quivering
- rapid eye movement
- rigidity
- crossed fingers
- chewing on things

Frustration, anger:
- making fists
- hands on hips
- stomping
- if sitting – on edge of chair (ready for action)
- chin out
- kicking the ground
- lips pressed together, jaw muscles tight
- running fingers through hair
- rubbing back of neck
- hand in pocket
- snorting
- clenched hands with white knuckles
- pointing or jabbing
- hot under collar

- putting out cigarette especially if with grinding motion
- change in skin color
- hostile stare

Defensiveness:
- hands in pocket
- hands behind back
- clenched hands
- men with jackets buttoned up
- folded arms (can be reinforced by making fists)
- crossed legs
- body twisted away, moving away, sitting back
- looking at door
- head tilted forward, possibly squinting
- stalling for time by cleaning glasses, rearranging, etc.
- hand rubbing back of neck.

Self–control, inner conflict:
- hand holding wrist or arm
- arm locked behind back
- locked ankles
- gripping arms of chair as in dentist's chair
- suppressed gestures or displacement activities such as fist clenched hidden in pocket
- hand to mouth in astonishment or fear (suppressed scream)
- hand rubbing back of neck, running fingers through hair (displaced hitting out), ``stiff upper lip'' or reacting as little as possible
- blowing nose and coughing (disguised tears)

Dominating:
- elevating self, like standing when others are sitting
- taking a different posture than others in a group, especially hands behind head
- sitting straddling the chair
- standing with arms spread and hands gripping desk or table
- loud voice or low voice carefully enunciated

- standing or walking with hands behind back and chin up
- thumbs in lapels

Superior and Subordinate:
- the superior usually has a hand on top in a handshake while the person who is subordinate offers his hand with palm up
- the superior makes the motion to terminate the encounter
- the superior can violate the subordinate's space and can express doubt, evaluation, domineering gestures
- the subordinate is more likely to signify self–control, anxiety, defensiveness gesture clusters
- when putting feet on the desk the superior should recognize that subordinates dislike this gesture, superiors pretend to ignore it, and equals take little note of it

Appendix B

"Open" and "Closed" Gestures

Our gestures often tell something about us that we are not able or willing to communicate verbally. Here is a partial list of "open" and "closed" gestures —"open" are present when a person is ready and willing to communicate, "closed" are present when there may be something standing in the way of honest, complete communication. These gestures can be observed in spousal relationships, parent–child relationships, supervisor–worker relationships, worker–client relationships, and any other time that two people are communicating. Maybe you will discover that your body language has been "telling" on you!

Open Gesture	Closed Gesture
open hands	hand covering mouth
palms up	making fists
unbuttoning jacket	peering over top of glasses
spontaneous eye contact	glancing at exit
smile	frown
leaning forward	leaning back
relaxed	rigid
hands away from face	looking at floor
standing straight	moving away
feet apart	legs crossed, shaking foot
shoulders squared	fidgeting
uncrossed legs	locked ankles

welcoming handshake	folded arms
touching	cold shoulder
patting	open palm tapping
rubbing palms together	hand wringing
affirmative head nods	head lowered
eye contact	lack of eye contact
calm use of facial movements	staring or eyes closed
body positioned toward other	rocking
seating arrangement with no barriers	stalling for time (light pipe, clean glasses, etc.)

Appendix C

Nonverbal, Silent Role–Play Activity
Directions:
Two people can do this activity, or it can be done in a group. It is similar to charades. Write down each of the following roleplay issues on an index card and shuffle the cards. You and your friend(s) take turns being the "speaker." The object of the game is for the "speaker" to illustrate the situation on the card using nonverbal cues only. The speaker is not allowed to talk. The speaker has a two–minute limit. The "listener(s)" are to guess what the speaker is saying after one minute has gone by and before the two-minute limit expires. Take turns until all players have completed a turn as listener and as speaker.

Nonverbal, Silent Role-Plays
Act out your:
- Attitude about the women's liberation movement.
- Attitude about the two major political parties in the United States.
- Attitude about the United States' manned space shuttle program.
- Reaction to the space shuttle Challenger explosion.
- Acceptance of the invitation to be a civilian astronaut on a space shuttle mission.
- Attitude about state lotteries.
- Reaction to accepting a lottery award of $1000/week for the rest of your life.
- Feelings about outlawing all ``happy hours'' at bars, lounges, and restaurants.
- Opinion on drunk drivers who get into accidents where bodily harm results.
- Attitude about legalizing marijuana.
- Feelings about the quality of TV programming today.
- Feelings about sex and violent crime on TV today.
- Feelings about TV regarding the younger generation.
- Feelings about how much TV a child should watch each

day.

- Attitude about the quality of movies today.
- Opinion on Americans idolizing movie stars and music personalities.
- Reaction to the current trend in popular music.
- Feelings about kids watching music videos.
- Feelings about popular music as it regards sex and the use of drugs.
- Thinking about the current trend in teenage clothes and hairstyles.
- Feelings about the passage of a ``Right to Life'' amendment to the U.S. Constitution.
- Feelings about mixing religious and political issues in the election of local, state, and national leaders.
- Feelings about the state of morality in America today.
- Feelings about the rise of ``fundamentalism'' in America today.
- Opinion on organized religion as it addresses the pressing issues of racial discrimination, world hunger, and bigotry.
- Feelings about the efforts of movie stars and music personalities to raise money for charity. (Live Aid, Band Aid, Hands Across America, AIDS Research, Farm Aid, etc.)
- Attitude toward letting others know your feelings.
- Feelings toward your family of origin.
- Attitude about the current problems in your marriage, in your family, on your job (or in school). (Three–part role play, two minutes per topic.)
- Reaction to getting a free trip to Disney World/EPCOT.
- Attitude toward the new/old Miami Vice fashion craze.
- Favorite types of music for listening, for entertaining, for romance, and for dancing.
- Favorite childhood story or fairy tale.
- Feelings about vivisection (animals used in laboratory research).
- Feelings about the way people get along at your place of business.

- Attitude towards support groups in regard to solving your current problems.
- Opinion about this game and the questions to be role played.

ABOUT THE AUTHOR

Connie has more than 25 years of building relationships with clients, building and developing teams and coaching business associates. Early in her career, she owned her own business for 10 years in North Carolina as a consultant and public speaker. For the past 11 years she has been a facilitator and coach. Connie has a passion for building, growing and developing business owners, teams and individuals.

Connie has been an IT Executive in roles like VP of Sales in Life Sciences and Healthcare. She earned her Regulatory Affairs Certification, Global by scoring in the top 96 percentile. Her background includes: Executive Coach for The Walt Disney Company. She was the Global Client Relationship Director for General Motors while with Accenture LLP. Prior to Accenture she was with Microsoft Corporation where she held the position of VP of Sales for the General Motors Account. In both roles, she had global sales and relationship responsibility for all of General Motors, their affiliates and subsidiaries globally.

Connie resides in North Carolina and owns Cwik Business Connections where she is a professional and executive coach. She enjoys spending time with her friends and family. She also enjoys golfing, reading and diy projects for her home.

www.ingramcontent.com/pod-product-compliance
Lightning Source LLC
Chambersburg PA
CBHW051326220526
45468CB00004B/1518